S I T E

Forest Building, Richmond, Virginia, 1978–1980, side
elevation and Terrarium Showroom, 1978, front and side
elevations.

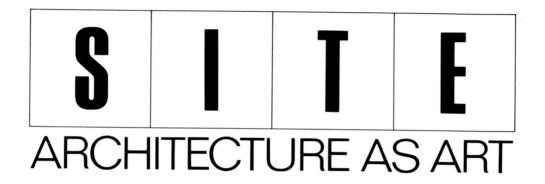

ARCHITECTURE AS ART

With Contributions by
Pierre Restany, Bruno Zevi and SITE

ST. MARTIN'S PRESS
NEW YORK

This book is dedicated to Sydney Lewis, Frances Lewis, Andrew Lewis and Mary Davis for their continued support and belief in our work during the past decade.

With special thanks to the Graham Foundation for Advanced Studies in the Fine Arts, the Samuel H. Kress Foundation, and the National Endowment for the Arts.

Photographs in this book by SITE courtesy Ronald Feldman Fine Arts, 33 East 74 Street, New York, N.Y. 10021.

For information write:
St. Martin's Press, Inc.
175 Fifth Avenue, New York, NY 10010

Library of Congress Number 80-54258
ISBN 0-312-04814-9

Printed and bound in Hong Kong

Contents

'In terms of general objectives, SITE has become increasingly committed to the sociological and psychological content of architecture, as opposed to problem-solving technology – or, described another way, architecture as art, rather than architecture as design. In answer to the controversy often raised among architects by this choice of priorities, the group has continued to point out that there is no implied forfeit of architecture's obligation to provide shelter and workable space. What this shift of emphasis does open up, however, is the possibility for buildings, (like theatre and literature) to begin to articulate society's subconscious responses to changing phenomena, instead of continuing only as a chronicler of its economic ambitions and fixed ideologies.'

SITE

SITE: Artists of Our Time

Pierre Restany

SITE outwardly presents itself as a living paradox in the panorama of architecture today, a paradigm of humor and disorder, the perfect antidote against Post-Modernist, Rationalist or Structuralist conventions. SITE style is the emanation of a state of mind, of an optimistic humanism based on the acceptance of the relentless flux of life and nature, far more than it is a tactic or a method; change (social, psychological, emotional, cultural) is the essence of reality.

In a world of fluctuating relativity SITE does not believe in 'permanent' architectural values but rather in the pragmatic virtues of human intelligence. To build means to adapt oneself to the relativity of a site, to create an autonomous object within a specific environment, yet an object that is necessarily subjected to the environment. The autonomous dimension of the built object turns it into a work of art, that is to say into a form of linguistic expression that substitutes information for metaphor, a critical dimension for passive integration. Form expresses itself in and for itself, it 'speaks' and it is self-sufficient in its meanings.

The renown of SITE comes from its 'showrooms' for Best Products, U.S. largest catalog showroom merchandiser, a nation-wide network of sales outlets, 40% exhibition space and 60% storage. It is on the basic functional shape typical of such outfits – the windowless box – that the active imagination of SITE has applied itself with bricks crumbling, angles blunted, parts of facades displaced. The spectacular aspect of this apocalyptic humor is obvious. No creation of SITE can go unnoticed: 'De-architecture', as its authors name it, is the tangible embodiment of the transitory and the ephemeral.

Each project obeys the laws of its internal logic. In a recent realization at Hialeah, Florida, the tropical vegetation is inserted into the structure: the facade is enclosed in a wall of glass; the space in-between contains specimens of the local flora. A continuous waterfall from the rooftop creates a fluid screen over the whole front of the building. This is a significant evolution, tending to present the built object as if it were a piece of the surrounding landscape. Now, the building no longer integrates nature, it is nature that integrates the building.

Such an inversion of logic works as a means of assuming the contradictions intrinsic to 'artistic' intervention, either functional or not, on public space: where does the art quality, the metaphoric quality and the critical quality of the whole begin and end? In the Ghost Parking Lot the parked cars are spread over with asphalt. The logical inversion reaches its culminating point: usually cars ride on asphalt. This radical option endows the environment with a mysterious beauty, and gives the forms a grave yet humorous touch.

One general observation sums up a project-by-project study. SITE attitudes constitute a socio-political commentary on the mores of our time. Architecture becomes 'subject matter', tool of knowledge, of criticism, or communication based upon the analysis of the motivations of the masses.

Nothing can alter the optimism of the group. Each project means a fresh start. While the Best showrooms have supplied a particularly favorable basic structural framework, other commissions will create other problems. We are into the real up to our ears, into a real that ignores any kind of fixation. Society will change and we'll change along with it . . .

At a time of Post-Modernist stagnation, SITE proposes a fresh look at the world around us: a humanistic ironical, open-minded look exempt of a priorisms. This type of outlook has strong affinities with the world view embraced by Marcel Duchamp after 1913.

The deviant functions of SITE lead to the other face of art, certainly not that of money, but of total openness to emotional change. Such a broad opening of the imagination at the service of human sensitivity needs to be sustained. That is a matter of culture, humanism and ethics. For SITE, the problem is how to remain faithful to its own style, its deviant function: direct in its ambiguity, logical in its contradition, ordered in its disorder whole in its fragmentation, determinist in its indeterminacy. These are the ingredients of a specific kind of humor, sometimes explosive, yet full of joie de vivre and of a realistic refusal to ignore the essential relativity of existence. SITE people are the real artists of our time.

Translated from French with the assistance of Michèle Cone

The Poetics of the Unfinished

Bruno Zevi

In a dramatic and almost grotesque fresco by Giulio Romano, in the Hall of Giants of Mantua's Ducal Palace, a Corinthian temple is violently broken into pieces, and its columns, arches and pediments collapse to the ground, devastating the whole obsessive scenery. It is the triumph of Mannerism. The primitive archetypes can no longer stand the political, social and aesthetic super-egos, embodied in the monumental, static objects of power: thus, in an apocalyptic dream, the symbols of classicism, the marble box and its iterative decorations, are destroyed.

There are many differences between the 16th century and our epoch. James Wines, Alison Sky, Emilio Sousa and Michelle Stone are not giants, and do not seem to be crushed by the ruins of our modern and much larger temples. However, when I first discovered their work, my thought went immediately to Mantua, to the profanation of the old Pagan world. In both cases, irony dominates. It is macabre sarcasm in Giulio Romano, while in the work of SITE it appears more cheerful. But to laugh in the Ghost Parking Lot of Hamden Plaza is an experience rather similar to that suggested by looking at the emphatic demolition of the Renaissance superstructures.

'De-architecturization' is their magic key-word. In spite of the great variety of applications, its meaning appears very coherent. In a project for Nevada, a bridge dives into the lake. In Venice, the facade of the Molino Stucky and the lagoon play together in a dialectic of inversion. In the Best showrooms, either the front or a corner or some other part breaks away, becoming an independent fragment or leading to an unexpected event. No doubt the results have a humorous connotation; but, behind them, there is a notable toil of inventiveness and critical intelligence.

Clearly, the polemic is against the 'finite' object. The notion of the 'unfinished' is very elementary. It was expressed in the Medieval and Baroque towns, where no building is complete in itself or isolated, but defines its own image through the integration of other components. The concept of 'finito' and 'non-finito' was technically formulated by Michelangelo both in his architecture and in his late sculptures. There are examples of unfinished urban plans, like in Ferrara, just as in houses of every period of the past. Frank Lloyd Wright, the greatest architectural genius of our time, spent his life fighting against the closed 'box' and preaching continuity. But architects do not seem to grasp that, in order to form an environment, interdependence between objects is necessary. Their buildings are monologues, and a lot of finite monologues produce neither traditional music nor Futuristic 'noises'. Pop Art has given us the instruments to perceive the cacophonous values of our wretched townscapes, but architects persist in the academic aesthetics of the self-sufficient building. In rare cases they double the box, as in Marina City of Chicago or in the World Trade Center of New York. What kind of dialogue may derive from two identical entities?

The Beaux-Arts approach has canonized the 'finite' ideology. To connect the ingredients of its stage-settings, it insists on consonance and symmetry. To find some rule capable of governing its revolting repetitions, it codifies proportion and perspective. While all formal details are analyzed in the most sophisticated way, living

Giulio Romano, *Collapse of the Giants' Hall*, fresco from the Palazzo del Tè, Mantua, 1534 (Alinari Art Reference Bureau)

man is totally forgotten. In the Beaux-Arts monuments, which include the Seagram Building and all Park Avenue towers and boxes, man can stand still, contemplating. Much the better if he is dead in a grandiose coffin. But, if he moves around, he becomes disturbing and out of tune with the eternal, immovable and universal surroundings. Believe it or not, there are people in the United States and elsewhere, walking freely in the streets and quite often even teaching at the universities or directing museums, who would be happy with another Beaux-Arts revival.

SITE's 'De-architecture' is an answer to the present state of foolishness, of cynicism and laziness. It is provoking simply because it offends academic common sense. It states that the finite building box, before being functionally absurd, is visually ridiculous. And gradually it erodes the building frame, in order to establish some contact with the environment. For instance, the top cornice brutally separates the building from the atmosphere above it; if a portion of the cornice is torn, the dialogue begins, because the sky penetrates into the building and vice versa. The side corners are other suffocating limits imposed by the frame; if one corner is broken up or flies away from the box, a dialogue is initiated between the inside and the outside space, between the lived-in cavities and the piazza or the street. As a paradox, the separation between a 'finite' arking lot and the 'finite' cars on it can be overcome by fusing the cars into the surface of the pavement.

n SITE's philosophy I see an extension of the most authentic American culture. It is heretical and realistic, at he same time. It recognizes and stimulates change at every scale, starting with the adjectives, the minor elements of architecture. They do not pretend to change society, they don't pose as prophets or reformers. Theirs is a caustic comment on things as they stand, but so amusingly corrosive that, after the comment, things do not stand quite the same anymore.

The original American contribution in the last two centuries is, one could say, SITE-oriented. It is enough to recall two aspects of it: Frederick Law Olmsted's urban conception and Wright's organic architecture.

Olmsted did not propose to eliminate the towns from the American territory, but he wanted cities different from the European ones, qualified by the frame of walls or greenbelts. In his vision, the built environment was supposed to merge with the natural environment, each incomplete in itself. The countryside would penetrate the built areas, somehow reaching the artificial, designed nature or the central parks. If we ask why Olmsted's city never fully materialized, one answer may be this: it did not find the proper language of an unfinished architecture that would give it a third dimension. Henry Hobson Richardson was looking for such a language, and this explains his friendship with Olmsted, but he died too soon, leaving the idea of an original American town in a state of suspense. However, in spite of the 'City Beautiful' (= neo-classical) movement, the American communities grew incomplete, fragmentary, full of missing parts, indeterminate. Vigorously undefined in their boundaries and skylines, fascinating and ugly, they embody the message of freedom from academic precepts. They are aleatory and sometimes alienating, but not fake. Only the architectural monuments like Lincoln Center in New York are definitely fake.

Organic architecture finds its origin in the same cultural context. Frank Lloyd Wright is the poet of continuity and change. He destroyed the building box by eliminating its frame: the lighting cornice of the Johnson Wax Administration Building in Racine, and the glass corners of his innumerable houses testify to this purpose. His masterpiece, 'Falling Water' at Bear Run, confirms it in an astonishing version. But Wright was a century ahead of his time. That's why everybody extols his greatness, then puts him in the Pantheon of geniuses and forgets his lessons.

In my opinion, the SITE group follows both Olmsted and Wright. Perhaps unconsciously, certainly in another key which fits in the wavering panorama of the last quarter of our century. What they reject – from the classicism of the International Style to the eclecticism of the so-called 'Post-Modern' – is exactly what Olmsted and Wright stood against. One may note that, in comparison with the skyscrapers and towers designed by Philip Johnson, Welton Becket, Minoru Yamasaki or Skidmore, Owings & Merrill, they have produced only miniatures. Well, the frescoes of Mantua's Hall of Giants speak to the public more directly than the thousands of Manneristic buildings which, in order to offend classicism, had to confirm its authority.

SITE – Description of the Organization

SITE is a multidisciplinary architecture and environmental art organization chartered in New York City in 1970 for the purpose of exploring new concepts for the urban/suburban visual environment. The buildings and projects of the group are a fusion of art and architecture which have been variously referred to as radical architecture, anti-architecture, arch-art, etc. However, SITE prefers the term 'De-architecture' as a general way of describing its philosophical position. De-architecture is a means or perspective for transforming the conventions of architecture and urban design through a process of inversion and the inclusion of certain social/psychological connections. For example, whereas the commonly sanctioned objective of 'design' has concentrated on a relationship between form and the internal motives of *use* ('form follows function'), the projects of SITE deal with a relationship between content and the external influences of context. Or, described another way, rather than develop buildings from the inside out, SITE's ideas evolve from the outside in. By shifting the emphasis from formal concerns to information and commentary, the projects of SITE reject the Modernist tradition of architecture as design in favor of architecture as art.

In addition to built projects, SITE produces a series of books on the environmental arts and architecture under the collective title *ON SITE*. These publications were initiated in 1972 as a resource for expanding dialogue in the public arts and for recording past and present activity internationally through the documentation of conceptual ideas, critical analysis, and built projects. The focus of both text and illustrations has been on non-formalist approaches to architecture and landscape by including such issues as indeterminacy, inversion, ritual, irony, humor, entropy, disorder, and social/political statement.

CURRENT SITE GROUP

Principals
Alison Sky, Emilio Sousa, Michelle Stone, James Wines

Associates
Robert Holmes, Peter Ruebel

Staff
Theodore Adamstein, Alan Baily, John Baumgarten, Laurence Jones, Michele Kaplan, Jewell McCarthy, Diane Maxon, Christine Morin, Patricia Phillips, Rafael Perozo

Notes on the Philosophy of SITE

The philosophical foundations of SITE began as a critical response to certain ideas and issues in 20th-century architecture – particularly the relationship between art and architecture. The first among these observations grew out of a dissatisfaction with the token role of visual art in the built environment. With rare exception, art has been regarded as a peripheral decoration of buildings and public areas and, consequently, our cityscapes have become punctuated by plaza sculptures and wall murals which exist more in the category of awkward intrusions than meaningful cultural resources. A second observation concerned the legacy of Modern design. Although this influential revolution of the 1920s created a new language of form based on function and technology (in opposition to the superfluous decoration of buildings associated with the 19th century), the continuous repetition of its vocabulary has left a widespread heritage of uncommunicative structures and spaces. For example, the most consistent popular reaction to architecture of the past three decades has been either total indifference or resentment because all buildings appear to look alike. Reinforcing this negative view of international Modernism, architectural critic Stephen Kurtz summarized in his book *Wasteland* that 'The processes of building – from those that produce its elements to those it shelters as a completed edifice – are such that it is impossible for human beings to derive satisfaction from them. To the extent that the final product reflects these processes, it reflects that alienation as well'. A third observation, growing directly out of the first two, focused on the question of why recent architecture has failed to communicate. The gap between popular interests and the messages expressed by buildings has been a tragedy of profound implications; but not necessarily the result of indifference or misguided intentions. Thoughtful architects, perhaps more than any other professional group, have maintained a high level of idealistic and humanitarian purpose. The problem has been their insistence on solutions defined exclusively in terms of architectural design. Paradoxically, there has been a direct equation between designers' utopian ambitions and the oppressiveness of the results. The more humanistic the intentions, the more modularized the answers. By limiting architecture to formal and functional definitions, the majority of the profession has avoided the complex responsibility of discovering new sources for a more relevant visual language, a language more in touch with a pluralistic and rapidly changing society. A fourth observation involved the interpretation of architecture as *art*, versus architecture as *design*. This question of art-as-opposed-to-design has been a semantic argument in this century which has never been successfully resolved. Architecture as art suggests *content*, whereas architecture as design favors *purpose*. Art is essentially a means of responding to the subconscious rituals and impulses of a social/cultural situation – usually as a compulsive and experimental activity, without practical objectives. Design, on the other hand, implies a priority of some useful nature to be accommodated on aesthetic terms – or, a compromise of art in deference to the expedient. Art is intrinsic and critical. Design tends to be applied and passive. For SITE, the notion of architecture as art has meant exploring a new iconographic role for buildings, based on the conviction that the ideas a structure generates as an extension of its own functions are neither as valid, nor as interesting, as those it absorbs from the outside.

In terms of architectural philosophy, the views expressed above have placed the work of SITE in a controversial position. However, aside from taking issue with certain academic interpretations of Modernism, the basis of these observations is securely rooted in the tradition and continuity of Western architecture for the past ten centuries.

One of the fundamental canons of Modern design, aside from functionalism, has been the aesthetic definition of a building as essentially a sculptural object – a result of the manipulation of form, space, and structure – and a dependency on abstract relationships as architecture's principal means of communication. When interpreted by the original masters of the Modern Movement (Le Corbusier, Mies van der Rohe, Louis Kahn, Alvar Aalto, and a few others), such physical ingredients as walls, entranceways, staircases, and windows achieved an intense psychological presence, beyond any specific symbolic associations. However, it occurred to SITE during the early development of the group's philosophy, that there is nothing inherently significant or meaningful about the abstract properties of cubes, cones, spheres, and cylinders – alone or in combination – which qualifies them to be regarded as the exclusive sources of architectural expression. As an alternative SITE postulated that, because the most communicative and enduring imagery of historical edifices was the product of social, psychological, cosmic, and metaphysical references, their structural confinement to plan and elevation was simply a concession to the responsibility for providing shelter and not necessarily related to the more important messages of a building.

When architecture emerged as an identifiable art form within historic civilizations, it was basically because all of the elementary technology of habitat had been resolved. Once the stability of walls and roofs was no longer a matter of doubt, the attention of past communities focused on ways to invest buildings with greater public significance. It was only logical that, since architecture served as the matrix for all of life's processes, it should be used as a form of media and as a way to establish places of special identity. When the various building types – houses, temples, palaces, etc. – had been resolved in terms of functional configuration, it became the duty of architects/artists to transform these edifices into celebratory events, into documentary records of popular ideals and consensus beliefs. Unlike Modernist designers who have tended to approach each building as a unique formal/sculptural challenge, these historical architects utilized existing typologies in order to imbue them with a universal social content. Or, described another way, instead of architecture developed from the inside out, Greek, Roman, Gothic, and Renaissance buildings evolved from the outside in.

The buildings and public spaces of SITE are an endeavor to incorporate some of the principles of these historical precedents and relate them to the contemporary urban/suburban environment – a context, it should be noted, lacking the consensus ideologies of the past necessary to produce a unified and coherent imagery. As a means of dealing with these inconsistencies and, at the same time, consolidating the group's philosophy, SITE began using the term 'De-architecture' in 1972. This theory is intended to challenge the notion of a building as the product of insular hypotheses by providing a perspective for examining these assumptions and expanding the definition of architecture. It is important to clarify the fact that De-architecture is but one of a number of philosophical viewpoints which emerged during the 1970s – each acknowledging that the present crisis of communication is a crisis of sources, each offering alternatives to the servile repetition of Modernist formulas. In order to explain De-architecture's basic premises and differences, it is necessary to briefly describe some of these other positions. For example, Post-Modernism has declared that architecture must be salvaged from the dehumanizing legacy of Modernism by the inclusion of anecdotal references to historical and popular imagery, by metaphorical allusion and a new plurality of sources. In this sense, architecture becomes a form of social intervention with a responsibility to identify and utilize whatever commonly accepted iconography the culture provides. Rationalism maintains that Modern architecture's obsession with formalism and functionalism has been limited to communicating the specialized interests of industrial capital, at the expense of the working classes and their particular needs and preferences. Often aligned with Socialist politics, this theoretical view proposes that architecture must be restored to its full ecumenical functions by means of a universal, classically oriented, language of form which can bridge class distinctions and accommodate all social change. And finally, Structuralism advocates architecture as a process of analysis of its own formal means, as a semiological study of underlying structure and 'linguistic relationships' in order to arrive at a better understanding of *meaning* (beyond obvious syntax and symbolism). In opposition to the use of allusion and metaphor, Structuralism deals with formal consistencies and the connections between 'signifiers' (surface structure) and 'signifieds' (deep structure or content). De-architecture represents an 'other level' of language investigation, but including certain aspects of these first three positions. This other level embraces the fact that an object – any object, including a building – can invade the subconscious without obvious reference to symbolic, metaphorical, and formal associations; but, instead, as a question concerning the identity of the object itself and whether what we see as that object even exists as perceived. Drawing a parallel with science, it has been repeatedly indicated by theoreticians that the human mind is a microcosm of the universe and that our inability to comprehend the total of phenomena is because we are the embodiment of the questions and not a vehicle through which the answers can be filtered. Yet science, like art, uses models of ideas to retain the comprehensible while exploring the incomprehensible. In this way the object (or model) and its associative meanings reaches beyond metaphor to become a point of connection between the human sense of limitation, on the one hand, and the notion of some abstract destiny, on the other. Viewed in a similar way, a building and its associative connections can be used as a point of reference (or a mental plateau) bridging the gap separating the known and the void. Without sacrificing any aspect of normal functionalism – in fact, making the condition of use itself into the raw material of art – architecture can (like theater and literature) articulate society's intuitive responses to a world of changing phenomena, rather than remain as only a chronicler of its economic ambitions and fixed ideologies. Quite simply, whereas the traditional criteria of Modern design has concentrated on form as an extension of function, SITE's theory of De-architecture favors content as an extension of context.

The basic purpose of De-architecture, in both its theoretical and built form, is to explore new possibilities for changing professional and popular response to the sociological, psychological, and aesthetic significance of architecture and public space. With these objectives in mind, the following statements are intended as a summary of SITE's particular applications of the concept.

Rather than treat art as a decorative accessory to architecture, SITE's work is a hybrid fusion of both disciplines, with the purpose of eliminating the conventional distinctions between art and architecture as separate entities.

For SITE, architecture is the *subject matter* or *raw material* of art, and not the objective of a design process. A building is usually treated as a given quantity, as a paradigm or typology, with all of its intrinsic sociological significance conditioned by habitual use and reflex identification. To completely re-create an architectural type – whether in the form of a house, civic center, or a market place – would, in SITE's view, destroy its more important associative content. Therefore, rather than impose a totally new design, SITE endeavors to expand or invert the already inherent meaning of a building by changing the structure very little on a physical level, but a great deal on a psychological level.

SITE's work rejects Modern design's traditional preoccupation with architecture as form and space, in favor of architecture as information and thought; a shift in priority from physical to mental.

One source of endless frustration for architects is the attempt to achieve complex formal and structural innovations within the restrictive realities of construction costs and real estate economics – a conflict of interests which usually forces architecture into a state of begrudging accommodation. SITE's work, on the other hand, accepts these practical limitations as part of an art statement and explores a visual language based on sociological observation, rather than compromised aesthetic.

It is SITE's opinion that architecture is the only intrinsic public art – all others, like painting, sculpture, and crafts, being only incidentally or by conscious choice a part of the public domain. Assuming that this public status implies communication to the largest number of people under the least exclusive of circumstances, SITE has chosen to work primarily in the most populated and commonplace of urban/suburban situations.

Traditional architectural iconography has been based on specific symbols which, by continuous repetition, reinforce the institutions they signify. SITE's imagery is a complete inversion of this legacy – reversing the appearance of institutional security and replacing it with a message of ambiguity and equivocation.

SITE's work often uses such phenomenological concepts as indeterminacy, entropy, fragmentation, and disorder as sources for architectural imagery. These concerns parallel, from an aesthetic standpoint, the scientific principles of relativity, dematerialization, and infinity. As an alternative to architecture's familiar celebrations of rational order, certain of SITE's structures suggest that a building is conclusive (and most intriguing) at that moment of its greatest indecision.

From all indications, a distrust of technological, economic, and political establishments appears to be one of the few consolidating forces uniting contemporary American society. A responsive architectural imagery, in SITE's view, should be a reflection of this disenchantment and a critical monitor of these declining institutions.

The term 'De-architecture' has been criticized as sounding negative; however, in a world where contraction and short supply will define the industrialized civilizations' options for the future, negation has become the philosophical equivalent of a new optimism.

In summary, SITE's philosophy is based on a commitment to the sociological and psychological content of architecture. Without forfeiting the practical needs of shelter, it is the objective of SITE to increase the communicative level of buildings and public spaces by drawing upon sources outside of architecture's formal, functional, and symbolic conventions.

In a world of disparity, indeterminacy, and change it has become meaningless for architecture to persist as a celebration of inflexible services or extraneous institutions – and, even worse, as a celebration of itself. We presently lack the cultural estate and unifying ideals necessary to sustain these early 20th-century principles with any degree of urgency or confidence. As an alternative SITE proposes that, if architecture is to regain its status as a meaningful public art, it should be questioned in most of its prevailing definitions in order to become more responsive to the diversity, complexity, and subconscious motivations of our pluralist society.

SITE

List of Buildings and Projects

1969 'Environmental Art Project', Metropolitan Opera House, South Wall Plaza, Lincoln Center, New York City (unbuilt)

1969 'Environmental Art Project', Everson Museum of Art Plaza, Syracuse, New York (unbuilt)

1970 'Education Place', University of Northern Iowa, Cedar Falls, Iowa (unbuilt)

1971–72 'Peeling Project', Showroom, Best Products Co., Inc., Richmond, Virginia

1971–72 'Physics-Astronomy Plaza', University of Wisconsin, Madison, Wisconsin (unbuilt)

1971 'Peekskill Melt', Crossroads Apartments, Peekskill, New York (unbuilt)

1972 'Binghamton Dock', State Street Park and Pedestrian Mall, Binghamton, New York (unbuilt)

1973 'Courtyard Project', Intermediate School 25, New York City (unbuilt)

1974 'Competition Entry', Society of the Four Arts, Palm Beach, Florida (unbuilt)

1974 'Platte River Rest Stop', Interstate 80, Nebraska (unbuilt)

1974 'Rest Stop', Interstate 80, Nebraska (unbuilt)

1974–75 'Indeterminate Facade', Showroom, Best Products Co., Inc., Almeda-Genoa Shopping Center, Houston, Texas.

1976–77 'Notch Project', Showroom, Best Products Co., Inc., Arden Fair Shopping Mall, Sacramento, California

1975 'Biennale Entries, Molino Stucky', Venice, Italy (unbuilt)

1976–78 'Tilt Showroom', Showroom, Best Products Co., Inc., Eudowood Shopping Mall, Towson, Maryland

1976 'Parking Lot Showroom', Showroom, Best Products Co., Inc., (pending)

1977–78 'Ghost Parking Lot', National Shopping Centers, Inc., Hamden Plaza, Hamden, Connecticut

1978 'Showroom Prototype', Best Products Co., Inc.

1978–79 'BEST Anti-Sign', Distribution Center, Best Products Co., Inc., Ashland, Virginia

1978–80 'Forest Building', Showroom, Best Products Co., Inc., Richmond, Virginia

1978 '341 Madison Avenue', Renovation Project, Vector Real Estate Corporation, New York City (pending)

1978 'Terrarium Showroom', Showroom, Best Products Co., Inc. (pending)

1978 'Water Gallery', Shopping Center, The Brandon Company, Miami, Florida (pending)

1978–79 'Hialeah Water Showroom', Showroom, Best Products Co., Inc., Miami, Florida

1978–79 'Cutler Ridge Showroom', Showroom, Best Products Co., Inc., Miami, Florida

Exhibitions

1973 Columbia University Department of Architecture in New York, N.Y. (six projects)

1973 Whitney Museum of American Art in New York, N.Y. (Binghamton Project)

1975 The Museum of Modern Art in New York, N.Y. (Best Houston Showroom)

1975 The Venice Biennale in Venice, Italy (Molino Stucky Project)

1975 Architectures Marginales Exhibition at the Pompidou Center in Paris, France (Best Houston Showroom)

1975 The Louvre in Paris, France (Best Houston Showroom)

1976 Experimental Architecture Exhibition at the CAYC Museum in Buenos Aires, Argentina (three projects)

1976 Illusions of Reality Exhibition at 8 museums in Australia (three projects)

1978 'Architecture – Service, Craft, Art' travelling exhibition at Rosa Esman Gallery in New York City, The New Jersey State Museum in Trenton, N.J., and the Muhlenberg College Art Gallery in Allentown, Pa. (four drawings – Houston, Forest Building, and L.A. Parking Lot Project)

1978 The Automobile Exhibition at Amerika Haus in West Berlin, Germany (Ghost Parking Lot)

1978 'Twentieth Century Ornament' exhibition at The Cooper Hewitt Museum in New York City (Ghost Parking Lot)

1979 'Buildings for the Best Products Company' exhibition at The Museum of Modern Art in New York City (six showrooms for Best)

1980 Ronald Feldman Fine Arts (gallery) in New York City (SITE exhibit)

1980 SITE Exhibition at The Virginia Museum of Fine Arts in Richmond, Virginia (construction environment, travelling show)

Bibliography

Note: Since 1970 there have been approximately 600 articles dealing with the projects and ideas of SITE in the architecture, art and popular press of 22 countries. This does not include international reprints of United Press International and Associated Press releases. The following list includes only articles of either feature length or special interest.

Published Articles and Criticism by SITE (for art and architecture reviews)

Art in America (U.S.A.), January 1970, 'Public Art, Private Gallery', by James Wines.

Landscape Architecture (U.S.A.), July 1971, 'The Case for SITE Oriented Art', by James Wines.

TA/BK (Holland), January 1972, 'Straatkunst', by James Wines and Nancy Goldring.

The Art Gallery (U.S.A.), March 1972, 'Peekskill Melt', by James Wines and Nancy Goldring.

Architectural Forum (U.S.A.), April 1972, 'The Case for the Big Duck', by James Wines.

L'Architecture d'Aujourd'hui (France), November 1972 'Le Point de Vue de l'Automobiliste', by James Wines.

Architectural Forum (U.S.A.), September 1973, 'Notes from the Passing Car', by James Wines.

Casabella (Italy), May 1974, 'Urban Art – Assisting the Assisted Readymade', by James Wines.

Kunstforum International (Germany), October 1974, 'Ent-Architekturierung', by James Wines.

A + U (Japan), June 1974, 'De-architecturization', by James Wines.

Architectural Design (England), June 1975, 'The Iconography of Disaster', by James Wines.

A + U (Japan), July 1975, 'De-architecturization, Part II', by James Wines.

L'Architettura No. 263 (Italy), June 1975, 'De-architecture', by James Wines.

Arts in Society (U.S.A.), Fall-Winter 1975, 'De-architecturization', by James Wines.

Modo (Italy), November 1977, 'Il Linguaggio Eretico della Dis-architettura', by James Wines.

Architecture Interieure/Créé (France), March and May 1978 (double issues), 'The Architecture of Risk', by James Wines.

Skyline (U.S.A.), October 1978, 'Architecture and the Crisis of Communications', by James Wines.

Art and Architecture Magazines

Art and Artists (England), October 1971, 'SITE'.

Architecture Record (U.S.A.), February 1972, 'New Concepts for Public Space Combine Art and Architecture', by Janet Bloom.

L'Architettura (Italy), May 1973, 'L'Intorno Scolpito', interview article by Bruno Zevi.

A + U (Japan), summer issue 1974, 'James Wines', by Toshio Nakamura.

A + U (Japan), July 1975, 'Indeterminate Facade', by Toshio Nakamura.

Deutsche Bauzeitung (West Germany), September 1975, 'Best Fassade'.

Architecture Concept (Canada), September 1975, 'La Façade Indeterminée'.

Domus (Italy), October 1975, 'Pre-disastro nel Texas', by Lisa Ponti.

Art News (U.S.A.), October 1975, 'SITE-ations', by Judith Goldman.

Art Direction (U.S.A.), February 1976, 'SITE', by Max Blagg.

Casabella (Italy), March 1976, 'SITE, Indeterminate Facade', by Franco Raggi.

Créé (France), December 1976, 'Désordre en Architecture', by Odile Fillion.

Kunstforum International (West Germany), January 1977, 'Fragment und Ruine – Provisorische Architektur', by Laurids Ortner (SITE projects on pages 99 and 175).

The Architectural Record (U.S.A.), March 1977, 'Bringing in the Business', by Gerald Allen.

Artes Plasticas (Spain), April 1977, 'SITE, Empresa Deconstructora', by Francesc Torres.

Nikkei Architecture (Japan), July 1977, 'SITE – Best Showrooms'.

Domus (Italy), August 1977, 'Fragmentation in California', by Lisa Ponti.

Architect and Builder (South Africa), August 1977, 'Integration by Disintegration'.

Design Magazine (England), September 1977, 'Wandering Wall'.

Bauen und Wohnen (West Germany), September 1977, 'Die Perfekte Schachtel'.

Arkitekten (Denmark), September 1977, 'Kunst Arkitektur, Anti-arkitektur, eller "De-architecture"?'.

Construction News Magazine (England), October 1977, 'Breakaway Architecture'.

Neuf (Belgium/France), November 1977, 'Perplexité de l'Architecture Americaine', by G. Luigi.

Architecture Australia (Australia), November 1977, 'The Drums Go Bang and the Symbols Clang', by Sydney Baggs (with commentary by James Wines).

The Architectural Review (England), March 1978, 'Through the Looking Glass', by Lance Wright (with comments by James Wines).

Data Arte (Italy), March 1978, 'E' tempo d'architettura', by Lopo Binazzi and Manfredo Tafuri.

A + U (Japan), April 1978, 'Notch Project by SITE', by Toshio Nakamura.

Architecture Interieure/Créé (France), May 1978, 'SITE Projects', by Olivier Boissière.

Bolaffiarte (Italy), June 1978, 'Il Parcheggio delle Auto Fantasma', by Francesca Alinovi.

Building Design (England), June 23 1978, 'Car Macadam', by Deborah Waraff.

Modo No. 15 (Italy), December 1978, 'New Haven, 1978 d.c.: Disco Orario di Pietra' by Franco Raggi (including interview with James Wines).

Ikebana Sogetsu (Japan), December 1978, (work of SITE discussed in context of an article on fragmentation in art).

Artes Visuales (Mexico), December 1978, 'SITE'.

Opus International No. 65 (France), winter 1978, 'Notch Project by SITE, Inc.'.

Impulse Vol. 7 No. 2 (Canada), January 1979, 'Works of SITE', (presentation of construction process and ideas related to projects).

Visual Message Vol. 1 No. 1 (Japan), January 1979, 'SITE – Three Projects'.

PT/Aktueel (Holland), April 4 1979, 'Openbare Bouwkunst Met Een Surrealistiche Tint'.

Techno Visie (Holland), May 2 1979, 'De Pop-architecture van SITE'.

Wohnen in Wien (Austria), June 1979, 'Architektur Ais Uverraschung', by Helmut Weihsmann.

Connaissance des Arts (France), August 1979, 'Une Esthétique de l'Incertitude', by Philip Jodidio.

Books and Catalogues

The Sculptural Idea (book), by James Kelly (U.S.A.), the Burgess Publishing Co., Minneapolis, Minn.; SITE projects discussed on pages 174–5.

A Proposito del Mulino Stucky, catalogue of 1975 Venice Biennale, Alfieri, Milan, Italy, 1975; SITE on pages 98, 99, 100, 101, 102, 103.

Unbuilt America (book), by Alison Sky and Michelle Stone (U.S.A.), McGraw Hill Book Co., New York, 1976; SITE projects on pages 254–5.

Kicked a Building Lately? (book), by Ada Louise Huxtable (U.S.A.), New York Times Book Co., New York, 1976; SITE projects discussed on pages 53, 56, 57.

Illusion and Reality (museum catalogue, Australia), Australian Gallery Director's Council, Sydney, Australia, 1977; catalogue for an eight museum travelling exhibition with two pages on the projects of SITE.

Esthetics Contemporary (book), edited by Richard Kostelanetz (U.S.A.), Prometheus Books, Buffalo, N.Y., 1978; inclusion of 'De-architecturization' by James Wines on pages 266–79.

Archigraphia, by Walter Herdeg (Switzerland), the Graphis Press, Zurich, Switzerland, 1978; SITE buildings discussed on pages 192, 193, 194, 195.

Architecture and Critical Imagination, by Wayne Attoe (U.S.A.), John Wiley & Sons, New York, 1978; SITE buildings discussed on pages 66–76.

Great Models, publication of the School of Design, North Carolina State University (U.S.A.), Raleigh, N.C., No. 27, 1978; interview with James Wines on pages 62, 63, 64, 65.

Coleccion Summarios (museum catalogue), 'Arquitectura Alternativa' by Emilio Ambasz (Argentina), Ediciones Summa SACIFI, Buenos Aires, Argentina, 1978; three pages on SITE projects.

Venerezia, by Pierre Restany, catalogue of the Venerezia Exhibition, 1978; Palazzo Grassi, Venice, Italy; 'Employment Project', Houston, 'Indeterminate Facade' and 'The Ghost Parking Lot' discussed on eight pages.

SITE Projects and Theories, by SITE, Dedalo Libri, Bari, Italy, 1978; overview of the complete work of SITE from 1970 to 1978.

Architecture and the Human Dimension (book), by Peter F. Smith, George Godwin Ltd. (the book publishing subsidiary of the Builder Group), London, England; SITE discussed on pages 129, 206, 207.

Selected Projects

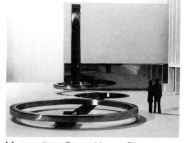

Metropolitan Opera House Plaza

Everson Museum Plaza

Metropolitan Opera House Plaza

Lincoln Center, New York City
1969

The first actual project commission received was for an environmental sculpture to be placed in the South Wall Plaza of the Metropolitan Opera House in New York City. This proposal suggested a large reflective wall of stainless steel which mirrored a series of horizontal metal structures, partially incised into the paving surface. Although still bound to formalist traditions, the intention was to create an environment based on reflection where the plaza, sculpture elements, and people would be seen in double image and, as a result, would appear to involve more space and activity than actually existed in physical reality. This project is significant mainly from the standpoint of representing an initial attempt at 'site-oriented' art. Although funded by the Adler Foundation in memory of philanthropist Louis Adler, the project was cancelled during its development because of the death of its principal patron, Mrs. Adler.

Everson Museum Plaza

Syracuse, New York
1969

Another early environmental art concept for I.M.Pei's Everson Museum in Syracuse, New York proposed a randomly poured metal 'distribution' piece which would visually fragment a large, rigidly formal, plaza space adjacent to the building. Although still identifiable as sculpture, the project introduced certain ideas of indeterminacy and undefined edges into the vocabulary of SITE's developing work. The proposal was never realized for lack of sufficient funds.

Education Place University of Northern Iowa

Cedar Falls, Iowa
1970

The proposal for the university space involved a 100-foot by 300-foot paving grid in grey and white checkered concrete, covering an undulating landscape configuration. The 10-foot modules comprising this grid were projected on various elevations, both raised and depressed in relation to the ground level. In order to create a sense of infinite flexibility, about 30 of these modules were designed as interchangeable and kinetic units incorporating such phenomena as light, sound, video, natural growth, and various other technical and material properties. These structures would have allowed occupants of the plaza to continuously alter their surroundings according to personal preference and seasonal conditions.

Peeling Project

Midlothian Turnpike, Richmond, Virginia
1971–1972

The 'Peeling Project' for Best Products utilized an existing showroom as the raw material of art. The facade was transformed by peeling the edges of the brick veneer to reveal a cement underfacing. The brick curving into space suggests an inversion of the construction process and generates an effect of architecture in a state of tentativeness and instability.

Construction Notes

The masonry walls of the building were composed of eight-inch load-bearing concrete block with a four-inch brick veneer. The existing veneer was removed and a new brick facade was constructed, reinforced internally with vertical steel rods and adhered with an epoxy-based mortar.

University of Northern Iowa

Peeling Project

Physics-Astronomy Plaza

Project Credits

Client: Best Products Co., Inc., Richmond, Virginia
Concept: SITE, New York, New York
Consulting Engineer: Mario Salvadori, New York, New York
Local Engineer: William J. Davis, Richmond, Virginia
General Contractor: Taylor and Parrish, Richmond, Virginia

34   a,b,c Drawings of structural details
      d Detail of peeling facade
35   View of the facade from the east
36   View of the facade from the west (photo John Henley)
37   Elevation drawing
      General view of showroom site
38–39 Views of the facade under construction

Physics-Astronomy Plaza University of Wisconsin

Madison, Wisconsin
1971–1972

In early 1972 a speculative project for the University of Wisconsin Physics-Astronomy Building Plaza was developed for the architectural firm of Fitzhugh Scott and Associates. The concept suggested a series of concentric ramps as a metaphorical embodiment of the Solar System. However, as in the case of the Iowa Plaza, the proposal included a broad participatory function and was not accepted.

Peekskill Melt

Peekskill, New York
1971

In Peekskill the site area included a middle-income housing project already under construction on a prominent street corner. It was the objective of the HUD committee to focus some favorable attention on this complex of buildings, since the structures had received criticism in the press for their unimaginative design. The committee hoped to salvage a negative situation by the inclusion of art. The SITE solution proposed 'melting' the bases of the brick apartment dwelling into the surrounding landscape by allowing the actual brick of the walls to flow over the adjacent ground surface. This 'relaxation' of an otherwise rigid structure was intended to alter the traditional relationship separating art, architecture, and site by unifying the three. Again, the project was never brought to realization. Ironically, it had been proceeding on schedule until an unfortunate notice in the press referred to SITE's idea as a decisive improvement on the 'mediocre architecture' (precisely the reason SITE was engaged in the first place), and the offended architect responsible for the building design persuaded the developer to abandon SITE's contribution as an unnecessary expenditure.

Binghamton Dock

Binghamton, New York
1972

The Binghamton project grew out of the special character of the environs (a riverfront community in upstate New York) and the need for a visual relief from the flat monotony of the town's Main Street and its unimaginative urban renewal. The site included an abandoned space between buildings, a connecting alleyway, and an adjoining shopping mall – in all, a total of six blocks of varied connecting parcels. The program called for the unification of these disparate configurations of space and architectural style. The final proposal suggested an un-

Peekskill Melt   Binghamton Dock   Courtyard Project, Intermediate School 25

dulating dock-like structure made entirely of locally produced heavy wood beams, remaining from years of pier removal after waterfront shipping declined at the turn of the century. The project articulated both land surface and walls and was easily perceived from a moving automobile on Main Street. When originally presented to the mayor and township officers, the dock concept was favorably received. The only reservations came from several HUD officials and from the local architect involved with the urban renewal. These negative influences finally succeeded in discouraging the mayor's council and the project was ultimately rejected.

Courtyard Project Intermediate School 25

New York City
1973

In early 1973 SITE was commissioned by the New York Board of Education to develop a courtyard for the new Intermediate School 25 designed by architect David Todd for Lower Manhattan. The concept by SITE proposed a dematerialization of the stairtower. The volume of this imposing concrete structure was to be physically reduced by gradually enlarging the size of the aggregate mix in the cement until the outward flow of the adhesive mass disintegrated into a casual distribution of stones and boulders at the far end of the courtyard. As in the Peekskill 'melting' building, the intention of the I.S. 25 inversion was to challenge the tradition of formal architecture as an inviolable object. Both projects suggested that architecture could become the 'raw material' or 'subject matter' for an art statement – a fundamental concept that became the motivation for most of SITE's subsequent projects.

Competition Entry The Society of the Four Arts

Palm Beach, Florida
1974

The terms of the Florida competition defined the site for the sculpture as a point at the end of a long grass island. As an alternative approach, the solution proposed by SITE utilized the entire land surface. A double wall of reinforced concrete splits the island from end to end. On either side of the split the earth is mounded to enclose the masonry structure. At the western end of the division the walls separate to expose a casual spill of stones and boulders gathered from the nearby waterfront. In a sense the land appears to have experienced an eruption at one extremity, while at the other end it seems to have closed in upon itself.

Platte River Rest Stop

Interstate 80, Nebraska
1974

The Platte River Rest Stop proposal for Interstate 80 incorporated the grass-covered gore area separating the highway from the recreation site. This strip was to be elevated in a series of gradually diminishing corrugations (achieved by an internal construction of pre-cast concrete). The effect of these undulating mounds and the ambiguous open space under them was intended to establish a kind of ritual environment in the flat landscape based upon visual access from a traffic lane.

The Society of the Four Arts

Platte River Rest Stop

Interstate 80 Rest Stop

Rest Stop

Interstate 80, Nebraska
1974

Developed as part of a Bicentennial Project sponsored by the State of Nebraska, the proposal by SITE was intended to be perceived by the motorist at high speed. The stenciled words REST STOP were to be painted on the roadway as through metamorphosized from the dotted roadway divider lines. Beginning several miles before the actual rest area, the letters would grow in definition until the words REST STOP were completely formed (about one mile before the site). Upon reaching the grass gore area, the letters would become three dimensional — beginning with the letter R and continuing in both two- and three-dimensional form. At the center of the gore the concrete letters would begin to drop away until they disappeared at the opposite end of the land surface. The stenciled highway letters would reverse as well and return slowly into the dotted paving divider. These reversed letters could then be read through the rear view mirror by the passing motorist.

40   View of the model and aerial view of site
41   Two views of the model

Indeterminate Facade

Almeda-Genoa Shopping Center, Houston, Texas
1974–1975

In late 1974 SITE began work on a project for a Best Products showroom in Houston, Texas. Unlike the earlier 'Peeling Building' renovation in Richmond, this facility was to be built as a new structure. It was decided, however, that the revised standard prototype (a 65,000 square-foot, two-story, white brick structure with pedestrian canopy) should be retained and that any contribution in terms of art should evolve from this basic reality. It was intended that the solution should serve as a com-

mentary on the proliferating high-rise boom of central Houston and also incorporate certain aspects of the grand Western tradition of false-front architecture.

The 'Indeterminate Facade' project completed in 1975 is a clear example of the fusion of the prototype into a different reality. The structure is an inversion of the standard merchandising warehouse located on a conventional shopping strip. The brick veneer of the facade and side walls has been arbitrarily extended beyond the logical edge of the roofline, resulting in the disconcerting appearance of a building arrested somewhere between construction and demolition. To intensify the ambiguity, a section of the central facade has been punched out and the waste bricks allowed to cascade over the top of the pedestrian canopy. Typical response to the showroom has been to interpret it as a symbol of apocalypse and/or destruction — or, as proposed by the French critic Pierre Schneider, 'The new American pessimism'. These metaphors are implied, but the intended dialogue is primarily concerned with missing parts, with the gap between the known and the void, with equivocation versus expectation as source for urban imagery.

In a paradoxical sense this reduction-by-construction is a reversal of Mies van der Rohe's famous maxim 'Less is more'. The inclusion of more (material) in the Houston showroom gives the impression that there is less (physical substance) and suggests that the intention of 'less' can be as intriguing an objective as the aspiration to 'more'. Or, as Marxist philosopher Georgi Plekhanov has suggested, 'Negative thinking is simply positive thinking moving in the other direction'.

Construction Notes

The Best Products Houston showroom was based on the corporation's prototype structure for 1975. To create the 'Indeterminate Facade', two of the exterior showroom walls were extended beyond their original parapet, adding a maximum of 27 feet to the 36-foot high showroom structure. In addition to working drawings, the masons were provided with a half-inch scale drawing indicating the specific contour of the facade and brick cascade.

The facade was constructed of brick reinforced with steel

Indeterminate Facade

Notch Project

and adhered with an epoxy-based mortar, and was engineered with a 200 per cent safety factor to satisfy local building restrictions.

To retain the spontaneity of the original concept, no mortar was used in the brick pile. These bricks were tested extensively in the wind tunnel at NASA, to insure that they were capable of withstanding winds of up to 200 miles per hour.

Project Credits

Client: Best Products Co., Inc., Richmond, Virginia
Concept: SITE, New York, New York
Architect: Maple-Jones, Architects, Fort Worth, Texas
Contractor: Conceptual Building Systems, Dallas, Texas

32	Members of the SITE team in front of the brick cascade (photo Robert Perron)
42	a,b,c Project sketches
	d Detail of the brick cascade on the facade
43	South elevation drawing and model
44–45	General view of showroom from the south-west (photo Michelle Maier)
46	View of showroom from the Gulf Freeway
	Detail of south-west corner
47	View from the south-west
	View from the south-east
48	Brick cascade under construction
49	The appearance of the facade at sunrise and sunset

Notch Project

Arden Fair Shopping Mall, Sacramento, California
1976–1977

The Sacramento 'Notch Project' is an extension of SITE's interest in fragmentation and subtraction in architecture.

In Sacramento, as in Houston, the standard showroom remains fundamentally unchanged; however, unlike the 'Indeterminate Facade' which includes additions as reductions, the California concept uses reductions as additions.

In the 'Notch Project' the main entranceway is a large, raw-edged gap removed from one corner of the structure. The corresponding positive, wedged-shaped unit is mechanized to open and close the showroom. This concept is an ironic commentary on contemporary public art and its token status as a decorative accessory – or, what the architectural profession so often refers to as 'integration of the arts'. The 'Notch Project' suggests integration by retaining the biographical evidence of a dis-integration which establishes a new relationship between art and architecture. When the Notch is closed the showroom exists as a simple warehouse distinguished only by its broken fissure. When open, it becomes both a building and a separate, but obviously related, 'monument'.

Construction Notes

The Best Products showroom walls are penetrated by a 14-foot high notch that serves as the main entranceway. The wedge, extracted from this gap, is mounted on a rail system incised into the paving surface. An internal electric motor and chain drive are located under the steel floorplate. The structural and mechanical members of the notch were fabricated, assembled and tested 200 miles from the actual building site, disassembled and then reassembled at the showroom. When activated, this mechanized 42-ton 'Wandering Wall' unit moves 40 feet in either direction requiring three minutes to open or close the entranceway. When open, the cantilevered second story and exterior walls are exposed, providing a shaded canopy area. The space between the notch and entrance functions as a shopping plaza – with the steel plate covered engine utilized as seating.

Project Credits

Client: Best Products Co., Inc., Richmond, Virginia
Concept: SITE, New York, New York
Architect and Engineer: Simpson, Stratta and Associates, San Francisco, California
Engineer for the Wandering Wall: Allied Engineering and Production Corp., Alemeda, California
General Contractor: Rudolf and Sletten, Inc., Mountain View, California

Molino Stucky

Tilt Showroom

Biennale Entries
Molino Stucky

Venice, Italy
1975

In 1975 SITE was invited to participate in the Venice
Biennale. The objective of this exhibition was the development of projects for the Molino Stucky, an abandoned
complex of grain mills on the Giudecca Island. The
municipality planned to restore these structures as a
community meeting and recreation center. SITE proposed
several solutions for the entranceway of the Molino facing
the Grand Canal, based upon the traditional Venetian use
of facade. Bearing in mind the overwhelming competition
with the architecture of the historic center, SITE's concepts were a series of inversions of this legacy. Two
theoretical ideas were based upon the canal/facade
relationship. One project addressed the eternal enigma of
Venice – whether the city has reclaimed the lagoon or
whether the lagoon is continuing to reclaim the city – and
suggested a series of nine reconstructions of the facade
elevation of the Molino, each gradually diminishing until
the final structure disappears under water. These fragments were intended to suggest an evolutionary process
arrested between various stages of growth and disintegration. The second proposal reversed the familiar interac-
tion between canal and facade by extending the prom-
enade as a horizontal replica of the vertical entranceway
of the Molino and by installing a massive water wall (a
glass-and-steel membrane supporting cascades of water
fed by a space frame) as the facade.

Tilt Showroom

Eudowood Shopping Mall, Towson,
Maryland
1976–1978

The 'Tilt Showroom', completed in October 1978, is an
inversion of the standard shopping center structure and
the architectural traditions of formalism and equilibrium.
The facade of the Eudowood Mall Best Products showroom is a casually tilted plane of masonry block which has
been created in response to already existing physical and
psychological circumstances. For example, since the
Towson site is a U-shaped retail center composed of
rigidly vertical and horizontal elements, the injection of the
Tilt is intended to establish a visual dialogue between this
routine situation and the precariousness of the facade.
The building is also a commentary on Modern architecture's obsession with form as the expression of
function. In this case the function is not expressed, but
simply 'revealed' by lifting one corner of the usual
impediment between client and merchandise.

Construction Notes

The showroom is a standard steel structure, with masonry exterior walls. The 14-inch thick tilting wall, composed
of structural steel and two layers of concrete block,
measures 202 feet by 38 feet, and has a total gross

Parking Lot Showroom

Ghost Parking Lot

weight of 450 tons. Its weight is transferred into the steel frame of the building through extensions of the structural members of the second floor and roof. The point at which the wall touches the ground acts as the stabilizing connection.

This building will eventually open into an enclosed shopping mall through the rear elevation. The tilting facade becomes both wall and canopy combined and the glass facade permits visual access to the showroom interior, and at some future date, to the interconnected mall beyond.

Project Credits

Client: Best Products Co., Inc., Richmond, Virginia
Concept and Architect: SITE, New York, New York
Structural Engineers: Weidlinger Associates, New York, New York
Mechanical Engineers: Scherr, Kopelman Associates, New York, New York
Electrical Engineers: Construction Concepts, New York, New York
General Contractor: The Whiting-Turner Contracting Co., Baltimore, Maryland

60	Drawings of structural details of the facade
60–61	General view from the south-west
62	West elevation drawings and general view of the showroom site
63	Tilted facade during construction and on completion
64–65	General view from the north-west
66	Opposing views from inside the tilted facade
67	View from the south

Parking Lot Showroom

Best Products Co., Inc.
1976 pending

This proposal to roll the central section of the parking lot over the building in a casual flow of undulating pavement,

is a complete inversion of the traditional relationship between architecture and site. The entire surface of both parking lot and showroom roof will be covered with asphalt, poured over a concrete supporting structure. In doing so, the relationship between what is traditionally regarded as building and space-around-building would become integrated to a degree where it would no longer be possible to discern where one began and the other stopped – suggesting that architecture need not necessarily be an object distinctly identifiable as separate from its context.

Consistent with the other projects for Best Products, this concept utilizes the materials and circumstances inherent in the commercial strip. In this case, two universal elements – the parking lot and retail warehouse (rhetorically condemned as eyesores by purist designers) are transformed into conditions of visual fantasy. The structure expresses the iconography of non-iconography in that it implies the elimination of architecture altogether; but as a beginning, not as a final requiem. The Houston Best showroom proclaimed its message vertically in the tradition of American false front architecture. The Parking Lot Showroom concept reverses this communication and conveys its statement horizontally. Additionally, the idea is a further exploration of SITE's intention to reverse the relationships between art and architecture and to expand the definition of both as they relate to public experience.

68	a Project sketches
	b Composite plan/elevation drawing
68–69	Two views of the model

Ghost Parking Lot

Hamden Plaza, Hamden, Connecticut
1977–1978

National Shopping Centers develops owns, and manages twenty major centers in the U.S.A. Under the leadership of President David W. Bermant, the company has pioneered in the development of this industry as well as in the use of art for the commercial environment. As an extension of Mr. Bermant's long-standing personal interest in

Best Anti-Sign

public art, National Shopping Centers has installed more than fifty examples by internationally known artists in its various facilities along the East Coast and as far west as Chicago.

The 'Ghost Parking Lot' inverts the relationship between two typical ingredients of the suburban shopping plaza – automobiles and asphalt – and establishes them within another frame of reference.

Twenty automobiles are enveloped by the paving surface on various graduated levels, from full exposure of the body contours to complete burial. The concept deals with a number of factors characteristic of the American mobilized experience – the blurred vision of motion itself, the fetishism of the car, indeterminacy of place and object – and utilizes them as the raw material for an art statement.

The 'Ghost Parking Lot' project, consistent with SITE's view of public art, employs existing physical and psychological circumstances in the development of a solution. Contrary to the prevalent use of 'object art' as a decorative accessory to buildings and public spaces, this project is neither 'placed' nor 'integrated' in any formal sense. Instead, it becomes part of its context by the inclusion of certain subconscious connections between shopping center merchandising rituals and the mythology of the American automobile. Also, unlike traditional public art conceived from the private art standpoint, SITE's Hamden Plaza project cannot be isolated or exhibited apart from its environment without a total loss of meaning.

Construction Notes

A group of twenty automobiles was acquired from area dealers and individuals. The cars were assembled in a local warehouse in Hamden and stripped of all interior fixtures, sandblasted to remove surface paint, and reinforced in window areas to withstand an infill of concrete. These auto body shells were then transported to Hamden Plaza and placed in a series of prepared excavations along the Dixwell Avenue end of the property. The cars were filled with concrete and the adjacent land surfaces modeled to absorb the contours. Exposed surfaces were sprayed with several layers of Bloc Bond (a fiberglass

strengthened concrete) in order to seal the metal surfaces and create the pavement 'skin' essential to the final aesthetic. The last stage included a layer of asphalt over the entire project and surrounding area to blend it with existing paving and re-painted parking lines to visually connect it to the rest of the facility.

Project Credits

Client: National Shopping Centers, Inc.
Concept: SITE, New York, New York
General Contractor: Depersia Masonry Contractors, Inc., Glastonbury, Connecticut

70	a,b Sketches
70–71	General view of parking lot and showroom from the street
72	Site plan and model
73–74	Four views of the parking lot during construction
75	Two views of the parking lot on completion

BEST Anti-Sign

Route 1, Ashland, Virginia
1978–1979

In 1979 SITE completed the 'BEST Anti-Sign' for the Best Products Co., Inc., Distribution Center in Ashland, Virginia. In this concept the company name is developed 'as' a wall, rather than traditionally located 'on' a wall. Using the entire facade and a portion of the side wall of the warehouse structure, this project involves the gradual transformation of the word 'BEST' by means of overlapping transparencies. The letters (porcelain on steel panels) begin as legible information and metamorphosize into an unreadable inversion of the entire premise for corporate identification – an anti-sign that is at once visible and invisible, positive and negative – within a seemingly endless continuum wrapping around the building. The Anti-Sign is 33 feet high and repeats the word 'BEST' for 525 feet (391 feet on the west elevation and 134 feet on the south wall of the Distribution Center). It is composed of more than 2,000 steel panels, which were covered with glass coating before being fired at 1,500 degrees fahrenheit.

Forest Building

Madison Avenue Project

Terrarium Showroom

Project Credits

Client: Best Products Co., Inc., Richmond, Virginia
Concept: SITE, New York, New York
Fabricated by: Ervite Corporation, Erie, Pennsylvania

76–77   Detail of the front elevation
78   Drawings of earlier proposals and view of 'Anti-Sign' wrapping around side wall
79   Two views of the 'Anti-Sign' during construction
80–81   Detail of the front elevation
82–83   View of the 'Anti-Sign' from the highway

Disintegrating Word

1978 alternative proposal

In this concept for an anti-sign, the applied letters forming the word BEST along the Distribution Center facade seem to be simultaneously emerging from and disintegrating into the building.

BBBESTTT

1978 alternative proposal

The tonal quality of the letters ranges from ten to 100 per cent black as they repeat along the facade, thereby creating an illusionary fluctuation in the shape and volume of the building.

Forest Building

Richmond, Virginia
1978–1980

This project, to be completed in 1980, will be located in a suburban site presently occupied by a dense forest. In a clearing area adjacent to a principal roadway there will be a parking lot; however, where the building threatens to destroy existing trees, the forest will be allowed to actually penetrate and envelop the showroom. This phenomenon will be hyperbolized by the surrounding asphalt, giving the appearance of architecture invaded and consumed by nature.

84   a,b Sketches of project variations
84–85   Model of proposed scheme
86   Aerial perspective and side elevation of the proposed scheme
87   Perspective drawings of project variations

Madison Avenue Project

341 Madison Avenue, New York City
1978 pending

The concept for Madison Avenue is intended to establish a new relationship between the neglected 'low-horizon' section of a high-rise building and its surrounding street activity. The project involves the renovation of an undistinguished structure located at a highly visible intersection.

Rather than propose major structural changes, the entire existing facade up to the first floor is enclosed in plate glass. At the street level, sandwiched between the glass and a plexiglass backing, a series of life-sized photos of people will appear in various stages of mingling, conversing, window shopping and walking.

The solution is intended to turn each of the standard renovation requirements into the 'subject matter' for a work of public art. For example, whereas the usual 'design' approach to renewing a building invariably destroys its original identity, this project hyperbolizes that identity by placing the entire facade in a showcase – or since display windows already exist, a showcase within a showcase, (like the cinematic device of the film within a film). Also, the concept becomes an ironic commentary on architecture's often proclaimed ideal of 'people space' in an urban setting. Instead of the familiar potted trees and concrete benches which generally fail to attract pedestrian activity, this project will start with a populated space; which, in turn, will initiate the dialogue between the building and the street activity around it.

Water Gallery

8   Two views of the site
9   Two views of the model showing proposed
        conversion

Terrarium Showroom
1978 pending

The 'Terrarium Showroom' will be located on a highly
visible plateau, near a major highway and surrounded by
mountainous landscape. This concept proposes using the
volume of earth excavated during foundation preparations
as the iconography of the finished building. The basic
walls will be made of cement block and the roof radically
inclined in a series of terraced elevations. A transparent
'skin' of 4-foot by 4-foot glass modules will enclose these
walls, allowing an 8-inch gap between glass and masonry.
This negative space will be filled with earth and rock,
approximating the actual terrain strata of the area, and the
entire roof will be covered with regional vegetation. The
general effect of the building will be similar to a geological
terrarium. The imagery of the 'Terrarium Showroom' is
intended to become a biographical record of its own
evolution, as well as a geological history of the California
region. Also, in time, as small plant life takes root in the
walls, the building will acquire a mutable iconography and
the community will be able to watch the structure 'grow'.

90   a,b Wall sections and partial elevation
        c Front, right, rear and left elevation
        d Plan
91   Right elevation, aerial perspective and wall
        section
        Sectional axonometric drawing
92   Perspective and section of wall elevation
93   Model and view of showroom site

Water Gallery
1978 pending

This water environment project is situated in a community
surrounded by ocean, with a near-surface water table.

The concept represents a unique combination of commercial strip architecture and the enclosed mall. In order to
communicate to roadway traffic, a 416-foot glass and
water 'billboard' defines the property from one end to the
other. This glass membrane is constructed of 4-foot by 4-
foot modules and the waterfall is provided by plumbing
units fixed along the top edge of the wall. All of the
shopping center's stores (including a Best Products
Showroom) are developed from a 4-foot module and
stationed directly behind the billboard. From the roadway
view, the sheet of water clinging to the glass wall will blur
the images of the stores and their identification signs,
creating the effect of an out-of-focus photograph. From
inside the mall, the water wall encloses the space and
provides a shield from the highway and parking lot.

Hialeah Showroom
5301 West 20th Avenue, Hialeah, Miami, Florida
1978–1979

The architecture of SITE is usually developed as an
extension of the sociological, psychological, and physical
characteristics of a particular context. In the case of the
Hialeah Best Showroom, the emphasis is on the relation
of the building to the roadway and to the natural environment of Florida. The entire facade of the structure
represents a microcosm of the surrounding landscape –
including water, vegetation, sand, earth, and rock. This
has been accomplished by enclosing the facade in a wall
of glass. This transparent skin supports a continuous
waterfall from the roof level and contains the landscape
elements. The resulting effect is intended to function as a
'living iconography'. Contrary to the traditional use of
sculpture and decorative accessories (which are ultimately static) on buildings, the imagery of the Hialeah Showroom is both mutable and evolutionary. From a visual
standpoint, the blurred impressions of the signage and
plant life, as seen through the refraction of the water,
emphasizes the kinetic experience associated with view-
ing the environment from a moving vehicle.

Hialeah Showroom

Cutler Ridge Showroom

Project Credits

Client: Best Products Co., Inc., Richmond, Virginia
Architect: SITE, New York, New York
Associate Architect: Johnson Associates Architects, Inc., Miami, Florida
Structural Engineers: Weidlinger Associates, New York, New York
Consulting Engineers: Milton Costello, P.E. Amityville, N.Y.
General Contractor: The Whiting-Turner Contracting Co., Fort Lauderdale, Florida

Cutler Ridge Showroom

19600 South Dixie Highway, Miami, Florida
1978–1979

The building is located on flat terrain, flanked on one side by railroad tracks and on the other by a main highway. This project is conceived to take advantage of both the long range visibility of the showroom from the highway and the more intimate relationship between the architecture and the pedestrians. The facade is segmented into four successive reductions which, together, add up to its sum total. The first section is the masonry and steel substructure of the showroom facade. The second is the front wall of brick veneer, situated about 10 feet from the front of the showroom. The third is extracted from the center of the second and incorporates the pedestrian canopy. The fourth reduction includes the three main doorways. From certain views these collective parts overlap visually in space and unify to create an appearance of the standard Best facade. From other positions when the fragments are seen disengaged from context, the building seems to be part of a surreal landscape – in some ways related to the odd juxtapositions and dreamlike qualities of a De Chirico or Magritte landscape. This effect is emphasized by the contrasting sun and shadow of the Florida climate.

Project Credits

Client: Best Products Co., Inc., Richmond, Virginia
Architect: SITE, New York, New York
Associate Architect: Johnson Associates Architects, Inc., Miami, Florida
Structural Engineers: Weidlinger Associates, New York, New York
General Contractor: The Whiting-Turner Contracting Co., Fort Lauderdale, Florida

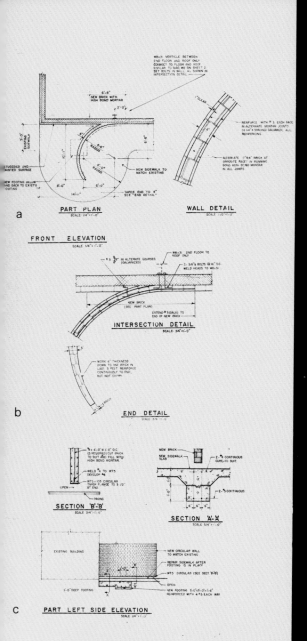

a PART PLAN   WALL DETAIL

FRONT ELEVATION

b INTERSECTION DETAIL

END DETAIL

c SECTION 'B'-'B'   SECTION 'A'-'A'

PART LEFT SIDE ELEVATION

d

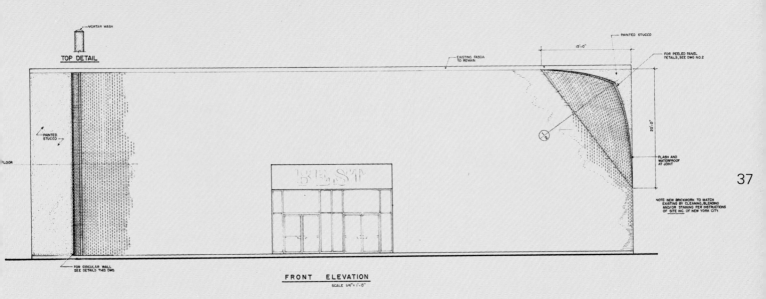

TOP DETAIL

FRONT ELEVATION
SCALE 1/8" = 1'-0"

37

38

40 Rest Stop

SITE, INC. 1974
James Wines

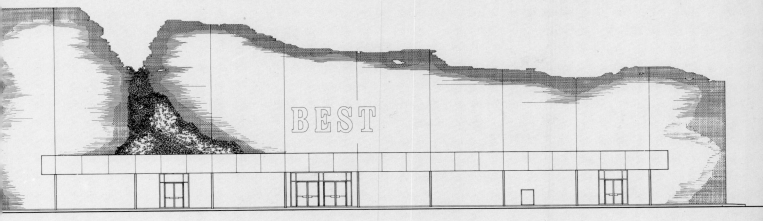

SOUTH ELEVATION

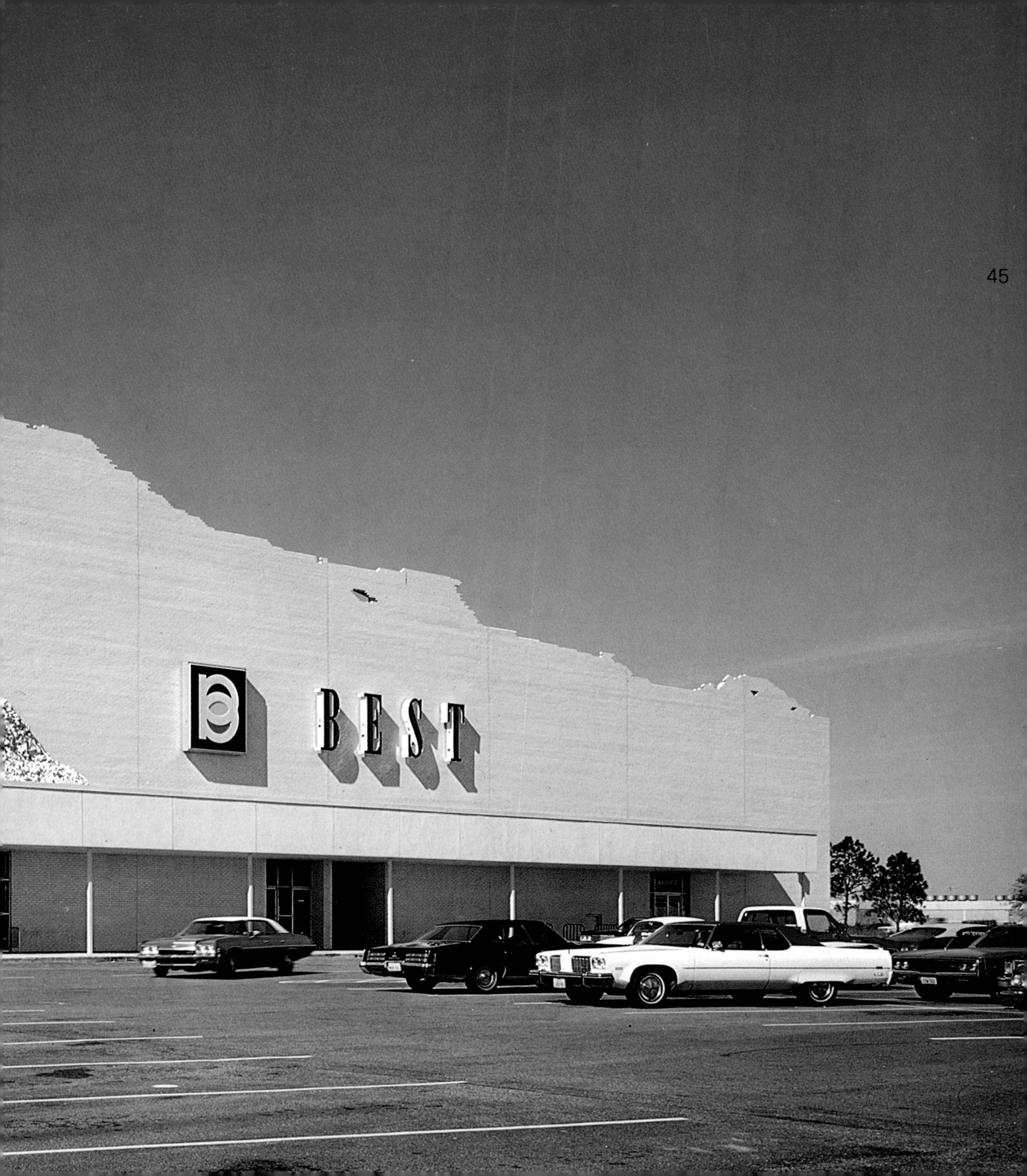
BEST

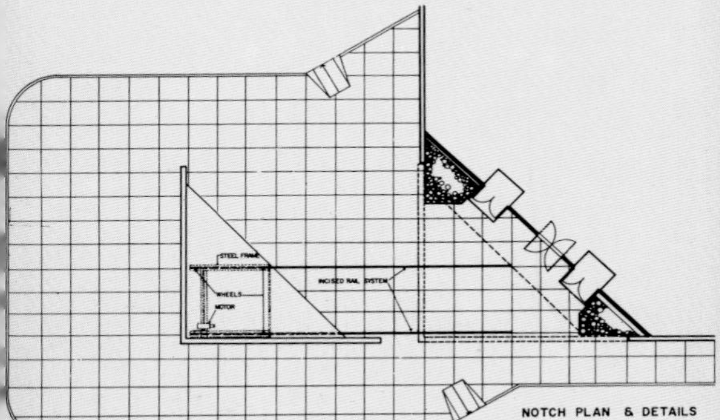

NOTCH PLAN & DETAILS

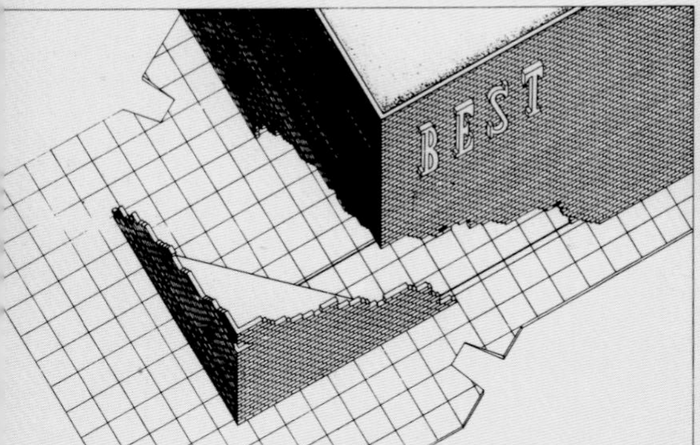

NOTCH ISOMETRIC VIEW

52

FRONT ELEVATION

54

LEFT SIDE ELEVATION

58 Molino Stucky

a

b

c

d

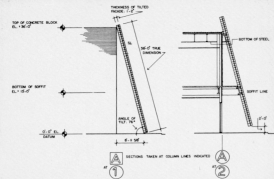

60 Tilt Showroom

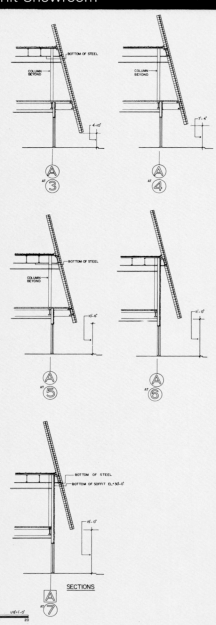

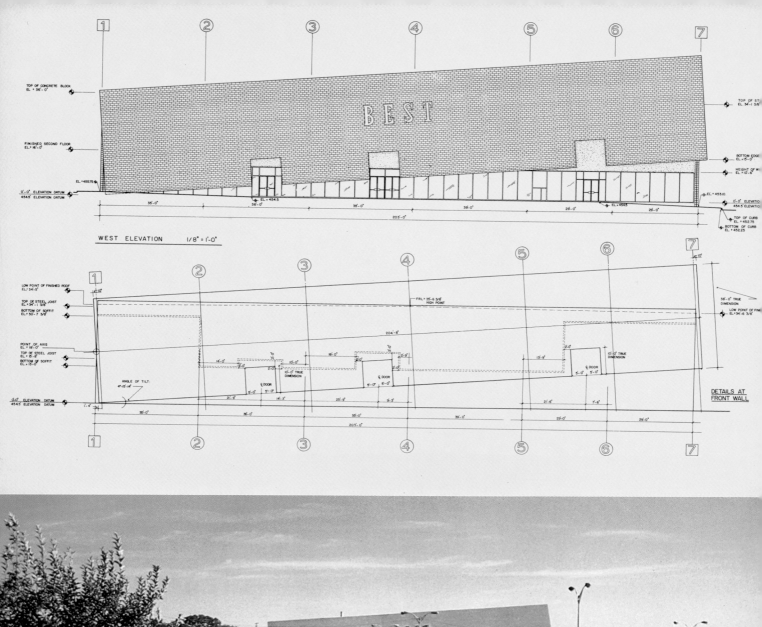

WEST ELEVATION   1/8" = 1'-0"

DETAILS AT
FRONT WALL

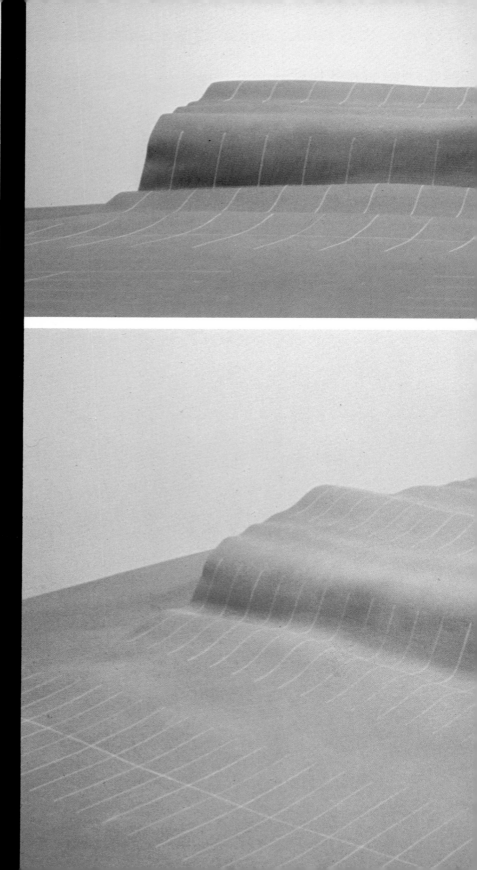

a

b

a

b

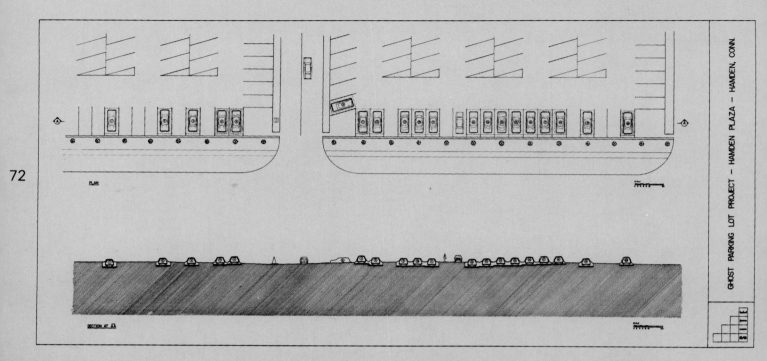

PLAN

SECTION AT A-A

GHOST PARKING LOT PROJECT – HAMDEN PLAZA – HAMDEN, CONN.

TITLE

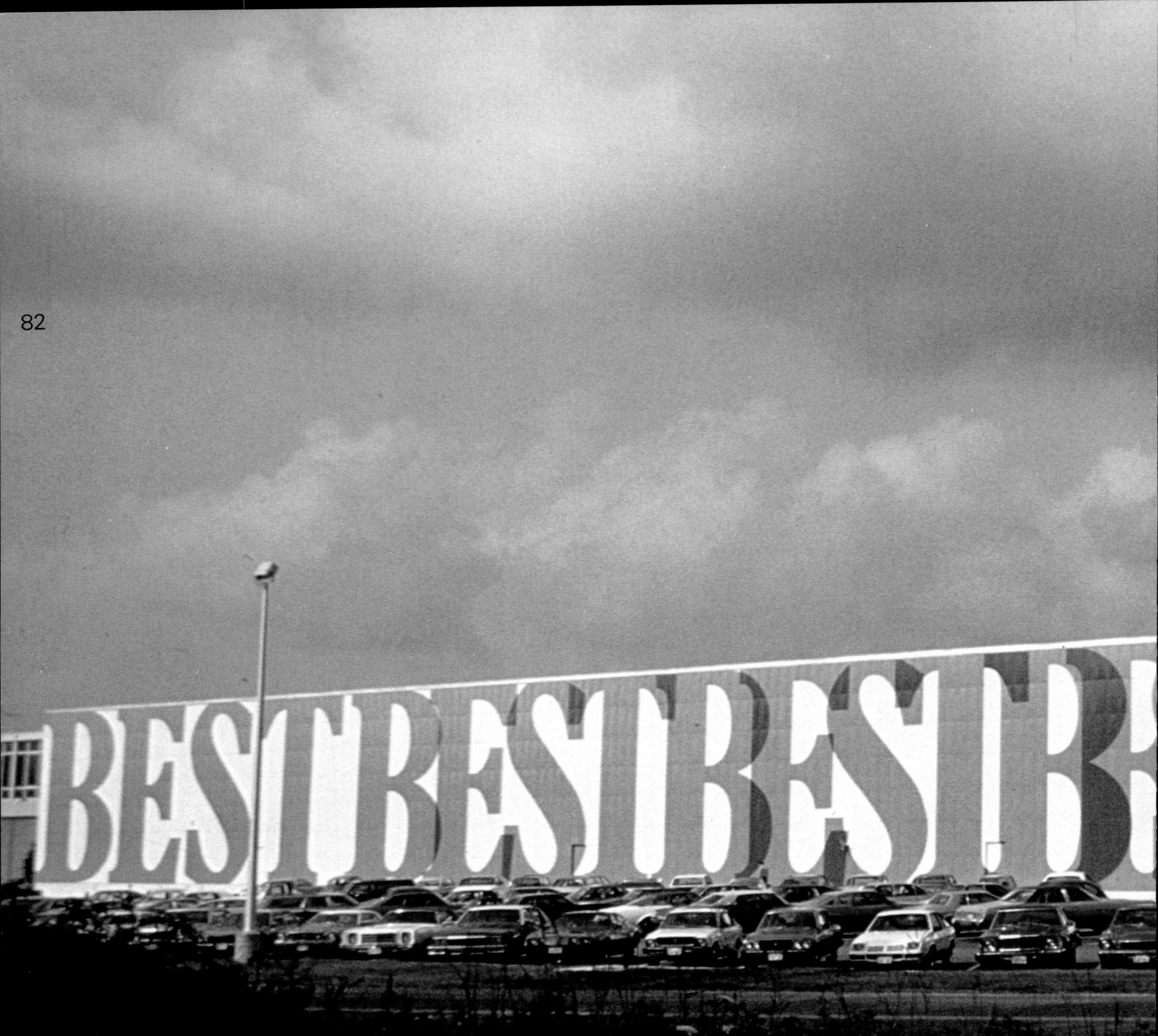
BESTBESTBEST

CATALOG SALES CENTER

a

b

Richmond Showroom – Best Products

SITE 56.
1978

RICHMOND SHOWROOM — BEST PRODUCTS

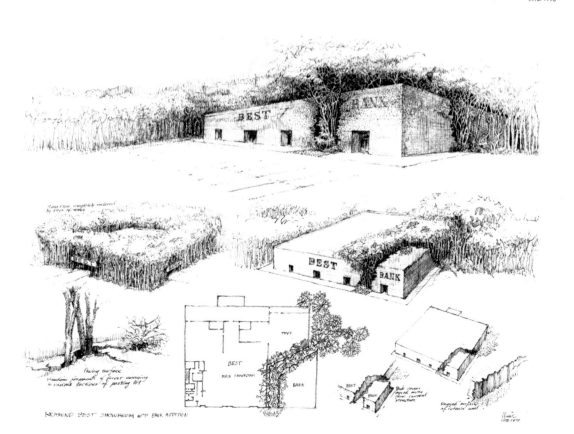

RICHMOND BEST SHOWROOM WITH BANK ADDITION

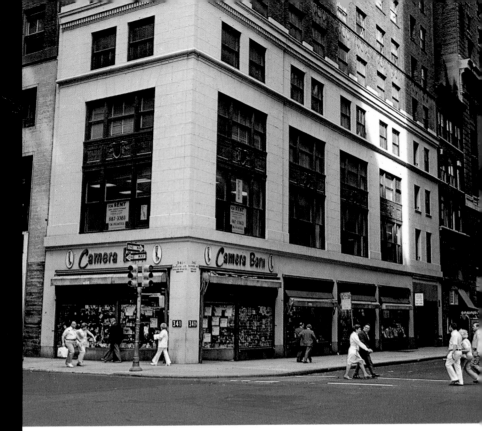

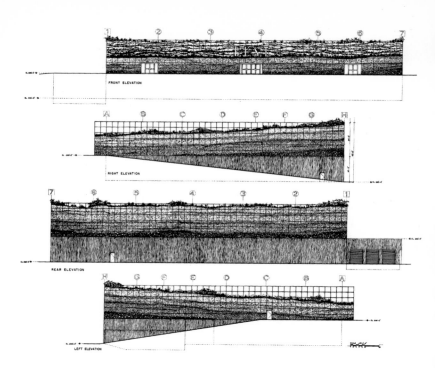

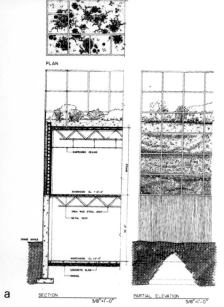

a

b

c

d

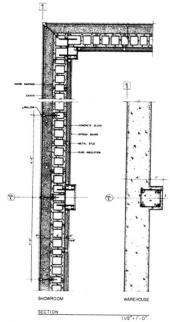

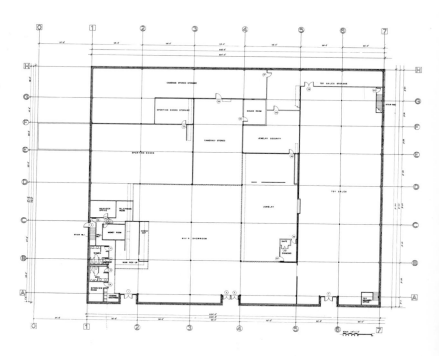

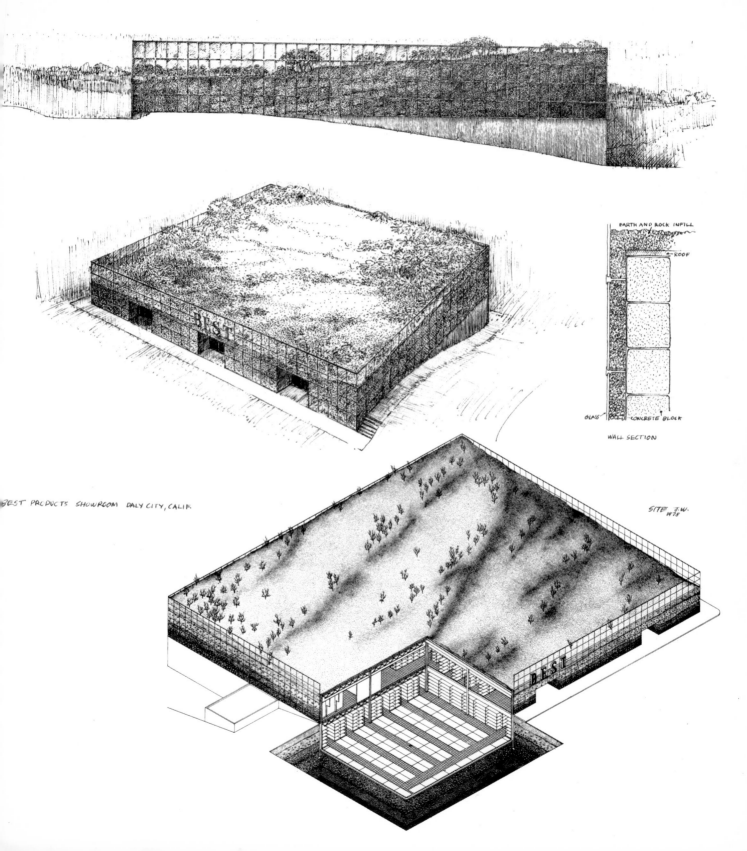

EARTH AND ROCK INFILL

ROOF

GLASS CONCRETE BLOCK

WALL SECTION

BEST PRODUCTS SHOWROOM DALY CITY, CALIF.

SITE J.W. 1978

a

WALL SECTION

3/8"=1'-0"

(labels): 3/4" COPPER TUBING WATER SUPPLY · TOP OF PARAPET ELEVATION - 37'-4" · PLANTER · METAL SUPPORT · GRAVEL · BUILT-UP ROOFING · INSULATION · 2"x6" STEEL COLUMN · 1/2" TEMPERED GLASS · ALUMINUM MULLION · 1/2" GYPSUM BOARD · 2" RIGID INSULATION · 8" CONCRETE BLOCK · 2"x2" STEEL SUPPORT · SECOND FLOOR ELEVATION +16'-0" · HUNG CEILING · 1/2" GYPSUM BOARD · 2" RIGID INSULATION · 8" CONCRETE BLOCK · CONCRETE RETAINING WALL · FIRST FLOOR ELEVATION 0'-0" · TRENCH DRAIN · RETURN TO PUMP ROOM

b

MULLION DETAIL @ STEEL COLUMN
N.T.S.

(labels): 1/8" STEEL ANGLE W/LEAD SHIMS TOP AND BOTTOM · 2"x8"x1/4" STEEL COLUMN · MULLION COVER · SILICONE BEAD · 1/2" TEMPERED GLASS

c

PLAN   1/4"=1'-0"
BEFORE INTRODUCTION OF
SOIL AT GROUND LEVEL

PLAN   1/4"=1'-0"
AFTER INTRODUCTION OF
SOIL ABOVE 6'-0"

(labels): 1/2" TEMPERED GLASS · 2"x8"x1/4" STEEL COL. · 8" CONCRETE BLOCK RET. WALL · TRENCH DRAIN · CONC. BLDG. WALL · 2" RIGID INSULATION · 1/2" GYPSUM BOARD · PLANTING · STRUCTURAL SUPPORT ABOVE

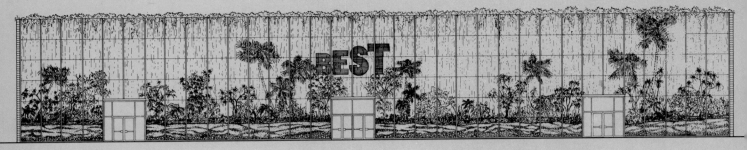

ELEVATION
1/8" = 1'-0"

BEST

BEST PRODUCTS CO., INC.
P.O. BOX 26303
RICHMOND, VA 23260
(804) 798-4211

HIALEAH, FLORIDA

S|I|T|E   SITE, INC.
            60 GREENE ST

PARTIAL ELEVATION OF
WATER WALL

SCALE: 3/4"=1'-0"

DATE
OCTOBER, 1979
DRAWN BY
P. RIESEL
SHEET NUMBER

R-2

102

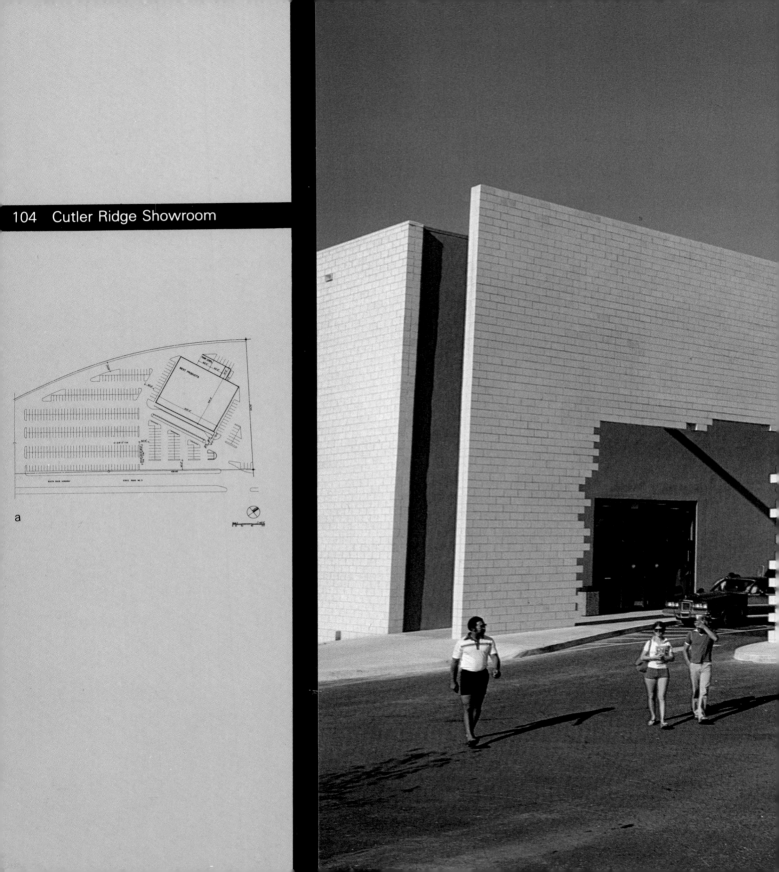

a

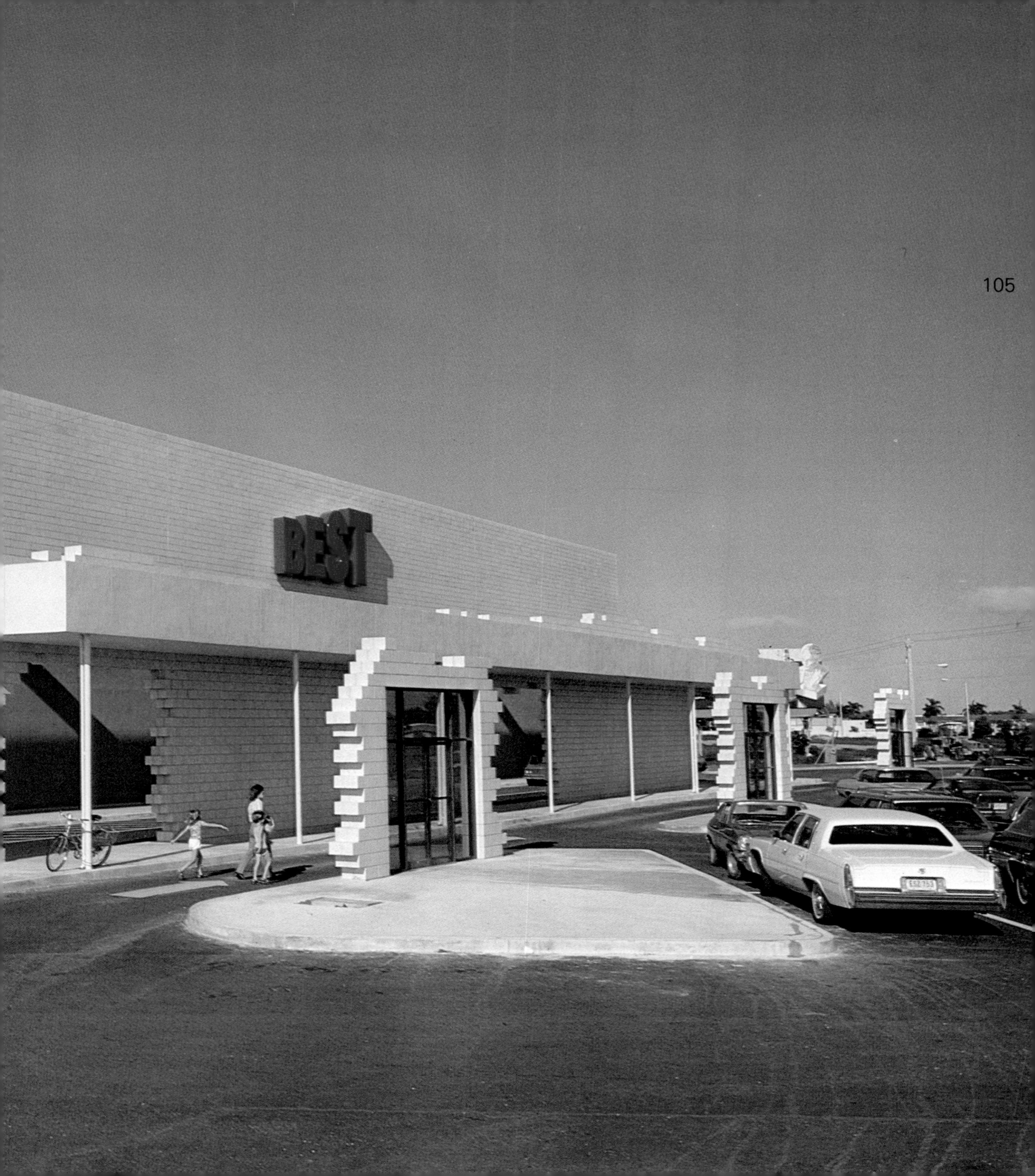
BEST

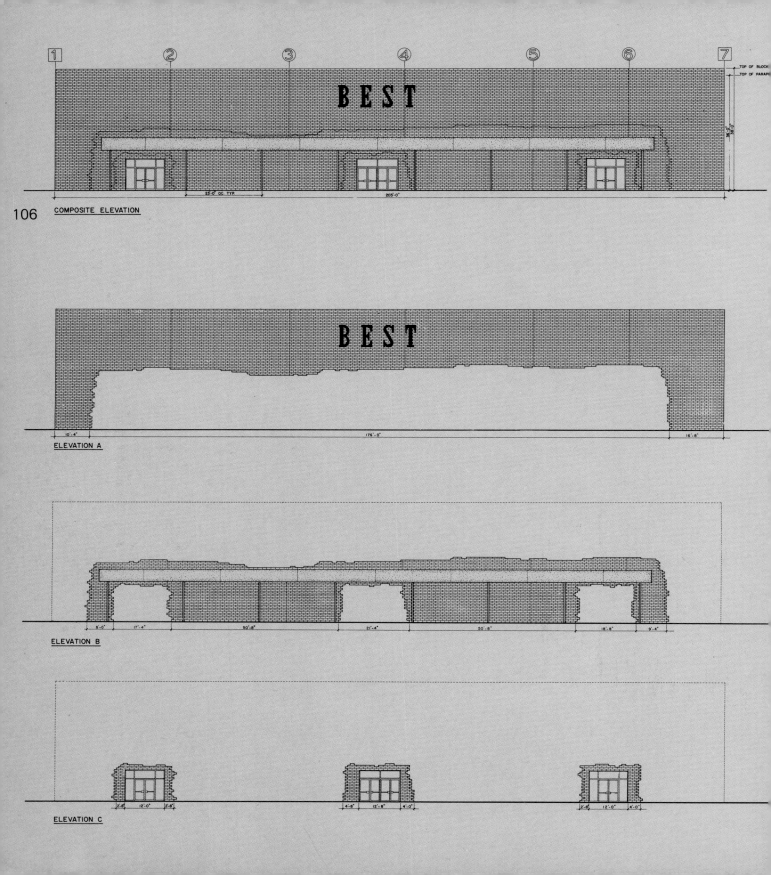

BEST

106 COMPOSITE ELEVATION

BEST

ELEVATION A

ELEVATION B

ELEVATION C